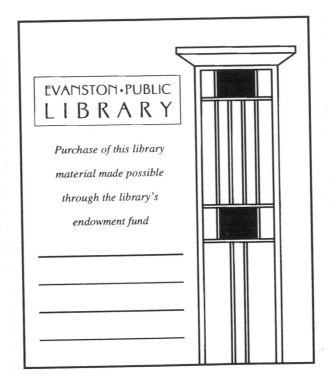

THE RISE OF
JIM CROW

DRAMA OF AFRICAN-AMERICAN HISTORY

THE RISE OF JIM CROW

by JAMES HASKINS and KATHLEEN BENSON
with VIRGINIA SCHOMP

VOTE FOR
CORDELL
ROBERTS

 Marshall Cavendish
Benchmark
New York

ACKNOWLEDGMENTS

The authors and publisher are grateful to Jill Watts, professor of history
at California State University, San Marcos, for her perceptive comments on the manuscript,
and to the late Richard Newman, civil rights advocate, author, and senior research officer
at the W. E. B. DuBois Institute at Harvard University,
for his excellent work in formulating the series.

——— A NOTE ON LANGUAGE ———

In order to preserve the character and historical accuracy of the quoted material appearing in this book, we have not corrected or modernized spellings, capitalization, punctuation, or grammar. We have retained the "dialect spelling" that was sometimes used by white writers in an attempt to reproduce the way some black southerners spoke. You will occasionally come across outdated or offensive words, such as *colored*, *Negro*, and *nigger*, which were often used by both white and black Americans at the turn of the twentieth century.

EDITOR: JOYCE STANTON   PUBLISHER: MICHELLE BISSON
ART DIRECTOR: ANAHID HAMPARIAN   SERIES DESIGNER: MICHAEL NELSON

MARSHALL CAVENDISH BENCHMARK 99 WHITE PLAINS ROAD TARRYTOWN, NEW YORK 10591-9001 www.marshallcavendish.us Text copyright © 2008 by James Haskins and Kathleen Benson All rights reserved. No part of this book may be reproduced or utilized in any form or by any means electronic or mechanical including photocopying, recording, or by any information storage and retrieval system, without permission from the copyright holders. All Internet sites were available and accurate when this book was sent to press. LIBRARY OF CONGRESS CATALOGING-IN-PUBLICATION DATA: Haskins, James, 1941- The rise of Jim Crow / by James Haskins and Kathleen Benson; with Virginia Schomp. p. cm. — (Drama of African-American history) Summary: "Provides a history of the decades of poverty, oppression, and terror that African Americans suffered under the system of segregation in the United States, from the end of the Reconstruction era through the early decades of the twentieth century"—Provided by publisher. Includes bibliographical references and index. ISBN 978-0-7614-2640-0 1. African Americans—Segregation—History—Juvenile literature. 2. African Americans—History—1877-1964—Juvenile literature. 3. United States—Race relations—Juvenile literature. I. Benson, Kathleen. II. Schomp, Virginia. III. Title. E185.61.H365 2008 305.896'073—dc22 2007034688

Photo research by Connie Garder. Cover photo by Hulton Archive/Getty Images: Back cover: Bill Hudson/AP Photo: Smithsonian Art Museum, Washington D.C./Art Resource; page 1: Mark of Shame , 2003 (oil & acrylic on board) by Bootman, Colin/The Bridgeman Art Library; page 2-3, : Doris Ulmann/Collection of New York Historical Society/Bridgeman Art Library; page 6: Digital Image (c) The Museum of Modern Art/Licensed by SCALA/Art Resource, NY; page 8: Art c Estate of Robert Gwathmey/Licensed by VAGA, New York, NY The Art Archive/San Diego Museum of Art/Laurie Platt Winfrey; page10: Bettmann/CORBIS; pages 12, 17, 19, 25, 46, 51, 53, 57, 66: CORBIS; pages 13,42, 47, 59 (top): North Wind Picture Archives; pages 14, 27: The Way Things Were, 2001 (oil on canvas), by Bootman, Colin/The Bridgeman Art Library; page 22: Private Collection, American School/Bridgeman Art Library; pages 16, 38, 60: Douglas Keister/CORBIS; pages 21, 71: The Granger Collection; pages 24, 31: SCHOMBERG CENTER/Art Resource, NY; pages; 28, 49 (bottom), 63, 70: Hulton Archives/Getty Images; page 35: Lewis Wickes Hine/CORBIS; page 41: Private Collection, French School/Bridgeman Art Library, page 44: Snark/Art Resource; page 48: R. Gates/Getty Images; page 49 (top): Schert/SV-Bilderdeinst/The Image Works; page 50: National Portrait Gallery, Smithsonian Institution/Art Resource, NY; pages 54, 59 (bottom), 67: Michael Ochs Archives/CORBIS; page 64: International News Photo/CORBIS; page 68.

Printed in China
1 3 5 6 4 2

Front cover: A young girl leaves a segregated coffee shop in the South during the Jim Crow era.
Back cover: Members of the Ku Klux Klan, an old-time white supremacist group that was revived in the days of Jim Crow
Half-title page: Chain Gang, by the twentieth-century African-American artist William H. Johnson
Title page: Mark of Shame, by Colin Bootman, 2003. A boy watches his father, who is unlettered, cast his ballot by signing his name with an X.

CONTENTS

Introduction 7

Chapter 1
THE EXODUSTERS
11

Chapter 2
THE BIRTH OF JIM CROW
23

Chapter 3
BEHIND THE COLOR LINE
33

Chapter 4
IDA B. WELLS AND THE ANTI-LYNCHING CAMPAIGN
45

Chapter 5
THE AGE OF ACCOMMODATION
55

Chapter 6
THE FAR HORIZON
65

Glossary 73
To Find Out More 73
Selected Bibliography 74
Notes on Quotes 75
Index 78

An African-American working man in the Jim Crow era, when segregation took firm root in the South

INTRODUCTION

The Rise of Jim Crow is the sixth book in the series Drama of African-American History. Earlier books in this series have traced the journey of African Americans from colonial times through the Civil War (1861-1865) and Reconstruction (1865-1877). Now we will explore one of the saddest periods in American history, the years from the end of Reconstruction through the beginning of the twentieth century.

Reconstruction had been a time of hope and promise for African Americans. Slavery was dead. The four million black men, women, and children who had won their freedom during the Civil War looked forward to a bright future in which they would enjoy the same rights and privileges as their former masters. At first, it seemed that their hopes would be realized. Congress sent federal troops into the former Confederate states to aid and protect the freedpeople. It passed laws guaranteeing basic legal and civil rights to all citizens, regardless of race. In 1867 black men cast their first ballots in elections establishing new southern state governments. Like the federal government, these Reconstruction governments were led by Republicans who favored broad social and political changes in the South.

Under the Reconstruction governments, the freedpeople made tremendous strides in their journey from bondage to true freedom. They worked to restore families that had been torn

Thousands of African Americans migrated from the South after the end of Reconstruction.

apart under slavery. They built new schools, churches, and other institutions. They formed political organizations and voted in record numbers. Southern black men served at nearly every level of government, from city councils to state legislatures to the U.S. Congress.

As they moved forward, however, African Americans also faced a host of barriers. White southerners overwhelmingly opposed Reconstruction. They resented northern interference in southern affairs, and they were horrified at the idea of former slaves enjoying the same rights as their former masters. Through a growing campaign of fraud, intimidation, and violence, whites strived to restore their dominance in the South. Members of terrorist organizations such as the Ku Klux Klan attacked thousands of freedpeople for asserting their rights. Black homes, schools, and churches were burned. Black men who voted or served in government were beaten and killed.

THE RISE OF JIM CROW

Those tactics helped the Democratic opponents of Reconstruction regain control of one southern state government after another. A federal crisis in 1876 made their victory complete. The results of that year's presidential election were so close that both Democrats and Republicans claimed victory. To resolve the conflict, the parties reached a compromise. The Democrats would accept the Republican candidate, Rutherford B. Hayes, as president. In return, the Republicans agreed to end federal intervention in the South. In 1877 the last U.S. government troops were withdrawn from southern soil. Without federal aid and protection, the remaining Republican governments toppled, and Reconstruction came to an end.

Historians have called the period following Reconstruction the "nadir," or low point, of African-American history. Restored to power, the former Confederates quickly erased all the gains southern blacks had made since emancipation. The freedpeople were subjected to a new and even more vicious campaign of violence. They were stripped of their civil and political rights and returned to a condition of economic dependence. The bright promise of Reconstruction faded into decades of poverty, oppression, and terror. The great African-American scholar W. E. B. DuBois summed it up this way: "The slave went free; stood a brief moment in the sun; then moved back again toward slavery."

Black sharecroppers labor in a white landowner's fields. This painting by American artist Robert Gwathmey was partly inspired by African art.

Chapter 1

The Exodusters

John Solomon Lewis was desperate. The Civil War veteran was working as a sharecropper in northeastern Louisiana, renting a small plot of farmland from a wealthy white landowner. No matter how hard he and his family worked, they could never seem to get ahead. "The man I rented land from said every year I must rent again to pay the other year," Lewis later recalled, "and so I rents and rents, and each year I gets deeper and deeper in debt." By the spring of 1879, the black farmer had seen enough. In "a fit of madness," he told his landlord, "It's no use, I works hard and raises big crops and you sells it and keeps the money, and brings me more and more in debt." Now, Lewis vowed, he would "go somewhere else and try to make headway like white workingmen."

THE SHARECROPPING SYSTEM

In September 1877 newly elected president Rutherford B. Hayes toured the South. Speaking to a large crowd in Atlanta, Georgia, Hayes assured the black members of his audience that their "rights and interests would be safer if [the] great mass of intelligent white men were let alone by the general government." To African Americans, the meaning was clear. The federal government would no longer protect the rights that had been granted them during Reconstruction. Instead, as one former slave put it, "The whole South—every State in the South—had got into the hands of the very men that held us as slaves."

African Americans knew exactly what to expect from such men. As southern Democrats had regained control of the Reconstruction governments, they had done everything in their power to restore the old slave system. More than a decade after emancipation, the majority of freedmen and women were working for white employers, under conditions that were not much different from their lives during slavery.

Worst of all was the system known as sharecropping. Too poor to buy their own land, most black farmers survived by working small plots owned by white landlords. The farmers entered into contracts with the landowners, agreeing to pay rent with a share of the crops

Farm families who were too poor to own a horse or mule had to plow their fields by hand. This photo was taken around 1890 in Savannah, Georgia.

they raised. After that share was subtracted, along with the inflated costs of supplies bought on credit from the landlords or white storekeepers, there was usually little or nothing left for the farmer. Like John Solomon Lewis, most black sharecroppers found themselves trapped in a cycle of ever-deepening debt and poverty. "Our old masters . . . make all the laws and own all the best lands," observed one Texas sharecropper. "We make as much cotton and sugar as we did when we were slaves, and it does us as little good now as it did then."

Hoping to improve their lives, many black sharecroppers moved on when their contracts expired. Most stayed in the South, moving from one plot of land and one landlord to another. Some traded the countryside for southern cities and mining towns. Others went even farther, relocating to cities in the North.

One of the few jobs open to a black woman was working as nursemaid to a white employer's children.

Whether in the South or North, African Americans who traded farm life for city life usually found more personal freedom and better educational opportunities for themselves and their children. However, they still faced the racial prejudice and discrimination that were woven deep into the fabric of American society. No matter how skilled or hardworking blacks might be, white business owners would hire them for only the most menial, lowest-paying jobs.

A large number of African Americans responded to these hopeless conditions by moving west. Following the end of Reconstruction, tens of thousands of southern blacks migrated to frontier towns in Kansas, Oklahoma, and as far

Southern black migrants seeking greater freedom and opportunity board a steamboat headed up the Mississippi River.

west as California. Many of the migrants were sharecroppers seeking an escape from endless grinding poverty. All were fleeing the racial discrimination and violence that were an everyday feature of life in the South. In early 1879 a black leader from Louisiana described the massive crowds of migrants lining the banks of the Mississippi River, clutching "their little store of worldly goods." Man and woman, young and old, all these hopeful migrants seemed to be united by one common belief: "*Anywhere* is better than here."

When John Solomon Lewis announced his intention of leaving the South, his landlord was furious. "If you try that job," the white man warned his tenant, "you will get your head shot away." So Lewis and his wife hatched a plan. In the dead of night, they took their four children and fled to a wooded area beside the Mississippi River. There they hid out for three weeks, until a northbound steamboat stopped at the landing. At first, the white captain refused the family passage. Lewis demanded his rights. "I am a man who was a United States soldier," he said, "and if I and my family gets put off, I will go in the United States Court and sue for damages." At that, the captain relented. Boarding the boat, John Solomon Lewis and his family began the next leg of their long journey toward a new home, where they hoped to find real freedom at last.

"SUNNY KANSAS"

TO THE COLORED CITIZENS OF THE UNITED STATES, trumpeted the headline of a notice published in black newspapers in July 1877.

> We, the Nicodemus Town Company of Graham County, Kan[sas], are now in possession of our lands . . . , and we are proud to say that it is the finest country we ever saw. The soil is of a rich, black, sandy loam. The country is rather rolling, and looks most pleasing to the human eye. . . . Now is your time to secure your home on Government Land in the Great Solomon Valley of Western Kansas.

Newspaper ads like this one, along with circulars distributed by hand and rumors spread by word of mouth, promised

All Colored People

THAT WANT TO

GO TO KANSAS,

On September 5th, 1877,

Can do so for $5.00

IMMIGRATION.

WHEREAS, We, the colored people of Lexington, Ky., knowing that there is an abundance of choice lands now belonging to the Government, have assembled ourselves together for the purpose of locating on said lands. Therefore,

BE IT RESOLVED, That we do now organize ourselves into a Colony, as follows:— Any person wishing to become a member of this Colony can do so by paying the sum of one dollar ($1.00), and this money is to be paid by the first of September, 1877, in installments of twenty-five cents at a time, or otherwise as may be desired.

RESOLVED, That this Colony has agreed to consolidate itself with the Nicodemus Towns, Solomon Valley, Graham County, Kansas, and can only do so by entering the vacant lands now in their midst, which costs $5.00.

RESOLVED, That this Colony shall consist of seven officers—President, Vice-President, Secretary, Treasurer, and three Trustees. President—M. M. Bell; Vice-President —Isaac Talbott; Secretary—W. J. Niles; Treasurer—Daniel Clarke; Trustees—Jerry Lee, William Jones, and Abner Webster.

RESOLVED, That this Colony shall have from one to two hundred militia, more or less, as the case may require, to keep peace and order, and any member failing to pay in his dues, as aforesaid, or failing to comply with the above rules in any particular, will not be recognized or protected by the Colony.

This 1877 poster promised African Americans an "abundance of choice lands" in Kansas.

rich opportunities in the western frontier. Under the Homestead Act of 1862, the federal government had opened public lands west of the Mississippi River to settlement. (The Native Americans who had long occupied those lands had been forcibly relocated to reservations.) The government would provide 160 acres to any "homesteader" who paid a small fee, built a home, and farmed the land for five years.

A number of African-American leaders encouraged blacks to leave "the rebel-ridden South" for western homesteads. Those promoting migration distributed advertisements, organized mass meetings, gave speeches, and formed colonization societies. The societies founded dozens of independent black frontier towns, including settlements at Nicodemus and Dunlap, Kansas. Thousands of African Americans, caught up in "migration fever," set out for those western colonies. Most of the migrants came from the states of Kentucky, Tennessee, Mississippi, Louisiana, and Texas.

The largest migration of the post-Reconstruction period became known as the Exodus of 1879, after the biblical story of the Israelites' escape from bondage in Egypt. During a few months in 1879, an estimated six thousand black men, women, and children left the South in a spontaneous, disorganized rush toward Kansas. The "Exodusters" were driven by fear of the "long pent-up hatred of their old masters," said one black Texan, "which they feel assured will ere long burst loose . . . and crush them if they remain here." They were drawn to Kansas by

THE RISE OF JIM CROW

Southern migrants pass through St. Louis, Missouri, during their long trek to new lives in the West.

promises both real and illusory. Black leaders including Benjamin Singleton, Henry Adams, and Edwin McCabe were portraying "sunny Kansas" as a land of opportunity, where African Americans could live free from racial injustice and terrorism. False rumors made the state seem even more attractive. According to one story, the government planned to set aside all of Kansas for the former slaves. Another rumor said that railroad companies were providing free passage to western train depots.

Many migrants left home with little or no money and only enough food to last their families a few days. Some walked all the way to Kansas. Some made the trek in wagons or by train. Most Exodusters traveled by steamboats up the Mississippi River to St. Louis, Missouri, then west along the Missouri River. However they traveled, the journey was long and difficult.

White southerners strongly opposed black migration. The cheap labor provided by the former slaves was essential to the

South's struggling economy. White employers, law officers, and armed mobs threatened, robbed, jailed, beat, whipped, and killed blacks who joined the migration movement. North-bound steamboats sometimes refused to carry black passengers to St. Louis. White merchants would not sell food to the Exodusters stranded alongside the Mississippi River. According to one newspaper account in April 1879, "nearly half a thousand" desperately poor travelers were left "without shelter, without food, with no hope of escaping from their present surrounding, and hardly a chance of returning whence they came."

All those obstacles slowed the Exodus but could not stop it completely. Despite all the risk and hardships, southern blacks continued to head for the western frontier. By 1881, an estimated 50,000 Exodusters had reached Kansas in one of the most remarkable mass migrations in American history.

Along with thousands of other black migrants, John Solomon Lewis arrived in Kansas with feelings of joy and optimism. "I looked on the ground and I says this is free ground," wrote Lewis. "Then I looked on the heavens, and I says them is free and beautiful heavens. Then I looked within my heart, and I says to myself I wonder why I never was free before?"

As soon as they landed, Lewis and his family held a prayer meeting on the banks of the Mississippi. They offered thanks for their safe arrival and prayed for loved ones left behind in the turmoil and violence of the South. "It was raining," Lewis recalled, "but the drops fell from heaven on a free family, and the meeting was just as good as sunshine. . . . I asked my wife did she know the ground she stands on. She said, 'No!' I said it is free ground; and she cried like a child for joy."

Exodusters pose
before their makeshift
cabin in the newly
opened Oklahoma
Territory.

In the "Promised Land"

The hardships did not end when the Exodusters arrived in
Kansas. Nearly two-thirds of the migrants could not afford
even the small fees required for claiming a homestead. Instead
of realizing their dreams of land ownership, they often ended
up working as unskilled laborers or domestic servants.
Migrants who did acquire land found that life was a struggle on
the western prairie. It took long hours of backbreaking labor to
raise crops in the dry, hard-packed soil. Drought and prairie
fires could destroy an entire year's harvest.

On top of all these challenges, black migrants often had to
endure the hostility of white Kansans who were overwhelmed
by the sheer size of the Exodus. In Wyandotte, on the Mississippi River, the white townspeople generously provided shelter, food, and medical care to the first arrivals. As the

Exodusters continued to pour in, however, the townspeople turned against them. In April 1879 a white delegation refused to let the captain of yet another steamboat unload his passengers at Wyandotte.

Black migrants also found that they had not left prejudice and violence behind when they left the South. Although racism was less intense in the frontier towns, most white Kansans considered African Americans somehow inferior and "immoral." In many areas whites would not allow their children to attend school side by side with black students. Black settlers might be threatened or attacked by white townspeople who feared that the flood of Exodusters would discourage white migration to Kansas. In Topeka a white mob tore down the new homes built by one group of black migrants, tossing the valuable eastern timber into the river.

Despite all these hardships, most blacks considered themselves better off in Kansas than they had been in the South. Over time about three-quarters of the Exodusters managed to acquire their own homes and farms. Black Kansans also established businesses such as hotels, blacksmith shops, and barber shops. They founded black schools, churches, and relief organizations. Although they did not enjoy the same civil rights as their white neighbors, there was far less racial violence and less interference with black political rights in Kansas than in the former Confederate states.

Following the Exodus of 1879, black migration continued throughout the western frontier. Between 1890 and 1910, African-American settlers founded about twenty-five black towns in the newly opened Oklahoma Territory. Black southerners also migrated to Nebraska, Wyoming, Idaho, Colorado,

Over time, many black pioneer families built a comfortable life on the western frontier. This family, photographed in the early twentieth century, settled in Nebraska.

California, and other western states and territories.

Even as these intrepid pioneers set out in search of freedom and opportunity, the vast majority of southern blacks remained close to their old homes. Unwilling or unable to migrate, these freed men, women, and children would face a difficult struggle against the rising tide of oppression sweeping the South.

WHITE

COLORED

Southern Jim Crow laws required the separation of the races in practically every area of public life, from schools to restaurants to water fountains.

Chapter 2

THE BIRTH OF JIM CROW

BY THE END OF RECONSTRUCTION, THE NORTH had grown weary of the subject of African-American rights. After years of upheaval, there was no end in sight to the constant struggles between the former slaves and their former masters. To most white northerners, there was only one solution. It was time for the federal government to step aside and let white and black southerners work out their differences.

For their part, most white southerners had never recognized the Reconstruction governments. Once Democrats regained control of the southern state governments, they quickly went to work dismantling the achievements of the Reconstruction era. Behind all their actions was a single goal: reestablishing white supremacy.

Southerners achieved that goal through the complex set of laws and practices known as Jim Crow. The Jim Crow system provided for the separation of the races. It created segregated

THE "REAL" JIM CROW

Thomas Dartmouth Rice performs his popular "Jim Crow" song-and-dance routine.

Come listen all you galls and boys
I's jist from Tuckyhoe*
I'm goin to sing a little song,
My name's Jim Crow.
Weel about and turn about and do jis so,
Eb'ry time I weel about I jump Jim Crow.

Those lyrics come from the song "Jim Crow," believed to have been written by Thomas Dartmouth Rice around 1828. Rice was a white performer in minstrel shows, a popular form of entertainment in the mid-nineteenth century. One night he created a new character. Dressing in tattered clothes and blackening his face with burned cork, he danced a comical jig while singing "Jim Crow." The performance was a hit with white audiences. Soon "Jim Crow" became a standard act in music halls across the North and South. The name became a racist slur, used to humiliate black men by identifying them with the ragged, clownish character. By the end of the century, the term "Jim Crow" also referred to the laws and practices designed to segregate and suppress African Americans.

*Probably refers to Tuckahoe Plantation on the James River in Virginia public services and facilities for blacks, which were nearly always inferior to those available to whites. From the end of Reconstruction all the way to the civil rights movement of the 1950s and 1960s, Jim Crow would strip African Americans of their political and civil rights, defining them as something less than second-class citizens.

THE ROOTS OF SEGREGATION

The Jim Crow system traced its roots to the Black Codes. These were laws passed in the South in the months following the end of the Civil War. The purpose of the Black Codes was to restrict the rights and freedoms of the former slaves. One of the first acts of the Reconstruction governments had been to repeal the Black Codes. (For more on the Black Codes, see volume 5 in this series, *The Reconstruction Era*.)

The South had another model to copy in creating the Jim Crow system: the discriminatory laws of the North. By the 1830s, slavery had been almost completely abolished in the northern states. Free black northerners enjoyed greater safety, security, and political rights than free blacks in the South. Like southern whites, however, most northern whites remained deeply prejudiced against blacks. Northern state governments devised a variety of laws to keep African Americans in their "place." In many states African Americans had to sit in the "Jim Crow" sections of railway cars, steamboats, theaters, and lecture halls.

The "colored" entrance of a segregated movie theater in Florida

They were barred from voting or serving on juries. They were educated in segregated schools and were forced to live in segregated neighborhoods.

During the 1880s, there was a brief flurry of opposition to the rising tide of racism in the North. Thirteen states passed laws protecting the civil rights of African Americans. In practice, however, those laws did little to end segregation. A Boston newspaper reported in 1899 that white supremacy was "now the policy of the Administration of the very [Republican] party which carried the country into and through a civil war to free the slave." A southern lawmaker put it more bluntly: "No Republican leader . . . will now dare to wave the bloody shirt and preach a crusade against the South's treatment of the Negro. The North has a bloody shirt of its own."

THE ASSAULT ON VOTING RIGHTS

While African Americans faced discrimination all over the United States, the Jim Crow system was most openly expressed, most far-reaching, and most often enforced through laws and violence in the South. The first step white southerners took toward installing Jim Crow was to suppress African Americans' political rights. Once southern blacks were barred from voting and serving in government, southern legislatures would be free to make segregation the law of the land.

The main obstacle to disenfranchising blacks was the Fifteenth Amendment to the Constitution. Ratified in 1870, the amendment made it illegal for a state to deny any male citizen the right to vote "on account of race, color, or previous condition of servitude." At first, southern whites skirted the law by threatening, attacking, and even murdering black men who attempted to vote. After Reconstruction ended in 1877, a variety of new tactics were added. Voting places were moved away from black population centers. The boundaries of voting districts were redrawn to eliminate black majorities in any one place (a practice known as gerrymandering). The process of voting was made so complicated that the large numbers of black men who were illiterate could no longer cast their ballots. In South Carolina, for example, election officials created special ballots and ballot boxes for each political candidate. A voter had to be able to read in order to match the candidate's name with the right box. If he made a mistake, his vote was thrown out.

Political cartoonist Thomas Nast takes a wry look at the literacy tests used by southern state governments to suppress black voting rights.

Beginning in 1890, southern governments set up new, more complicated barriers for voters. Every citizen was required to pay a fee known as a poll tax before registering to vote. He had to meet property and residency requirements, proving that he owned a sufficient amount of land and had lived in one place for several years. He also had to pass a literacy test, answering difficult questions about the meaning of a state's constitution. Loopholes in all these requirements allowed local election officials to "pass" poor and illiterate white voters while disqualifying blacks.

The tactics for disenfranchising southern blacks were highly effective. In Georgia and South Carolina, the number of black

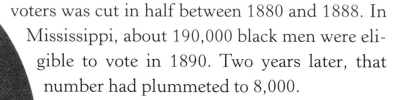

voters was cut in half between 1880 and 1888. In Mississippi, about 190,000 black men were eligible to vote in 1890. Two years later, that number had plummeted to 8,000.

As black southerners lost their voting rights, black elected officials also faded away. George H. White, whose term as a representative from North Carolina ended in 1901, was the last African American to serve in Congress for more than two decades. In his farewell address, White declared that blacks had made great progress against overwhelming odds since emancipation. The black man "asks no special favors," he told fellow congressmen,

George H. White, representative from North Carolina, was the last former slave to serve in Congress.

but simply demands that he be given the same chance for existence, for earning a livelihood, for raising himself in the scales of manhood and womanhood that are accorded to kindred nationalities. . . . This [speech] . . . is perhaps the negroes' temporary farewell to the American Congress; but let me say, . . . he will rise up some day and come again.

PLESSY V. FERGUSON

The first Jim Crow laws in the South related to public transportation. In 1881 Tennessee passed a law requiring railroads to provide separate coaches for black and white passengers. Eight other southern states soon followed. An editorial in a white New Orleans newspaper explained why Louisiana needed its own railway segregation law.

The law . . . which prohibits the negroes from occupying the same place in a hotel, restaurant or theatre as the whites, should prevail as to [railroad] cars also. Whites and blacks may there be crowded together, squeezed close to each other in the same seats. . . . A man that would be horrified at the idea of his wife or daughter seated by the side of a burly negro in the parlor of a hotel or at a restaurant cannot see her occupying a crowded seat in a car next to a negro without the same feeling of disgust.

Louisiana's Separate Car Act was signed into law in 1890. A year later, a black citizens' committee in New Orleans decided to challenge the discriminatory law. Homer Plessy, a young black man who was so light-skinned that he could "pass" for white, bought a first-class train ticket. Plessy sat down in the whites-only car. When the conductor (who was working with the committee) asked his race, he replied, "I am a colored man." The conductor told Plessy that he would have to move to the "colored car." The young man refused, and he was arrested.

Albion Tourgée, a white northern civil rights lawyer, argued Plessy's case in a New Orleans court. Judge John H. Ferguson found the young man guilty of violating the Separate Car Law. Tourgée appealed Ferguson's ruling all the way to the U.S. Supreme Court. In April 1896 the lawyer presented his case. Tourgée argued that the Separate Car Law violated a clause of the Fourteenth Amendment that guaranteed citizens equal protection under the law. The "real object" of the Louisiana law was "to keep Negroes out of one car for the gratification of whites."

Instead of treating all its citizens equally, Tourgée argued, Louisiana was declaring that blacks were inferior to whites.

The Supreme Court disagreed. In its ruling it rejected the idea that

> the enforced separation of the two races stamps the colored race with a badge of inferiority. If this be so, it is not by reason of anything found in the act, but solely because the colored race chooses to put that construction on it. . . . If one race be inferior to the other socially, the constitution of the United States cannot put them on the same plane.

In other words, the court ruled that the Fourteenth Amendment did not seek to guarantee the social equality of all races. That was something outside the scope of the law. Separation of the races was legal, then, as long as states made an effort to provide equal facilities for whites and blacks.

The Supreme Court's decision in the case of *Plessy* v. *Ferguson* established the "separate but equal" doctrine. Emboldened by the ruling, state and local governments throughout the South would pass laws expanding segregation into almost every area of public life. As long as lawmakers claimed that the facilities for blacks and whites were roughly equal, African Americans had no hope of overturning the Jim Crow laws. In reality, conditions for blacks were nearly always separate but almost never equal.

A LONELY VOICE

The ruling in *Plessy* v. *Ferguson* was just one of dozens of Supreme Court decisions that whittled away at African-American rights in the Jim Crow era. Supreme Court Justice John Marshall Harlan became known as the "great dissenter" for his record of opposing those rulings. Harlan was the only justice who spoke out against the majority decision in the Plessy case. A half century later, his passionate dissent would serve as an inspiration to lawyers challenging segregation during the civil rights movement.

> In view of the constitution, in the eye of the law, there is in this country no superior, dominant, ruling class of citizens. . . . The destinies of the two races, in this country, are indissolubly linked together, and the interests of both require that the common government of all shall not permit the seeds of race hate to be planted under the sanction of law. . . . We boast of the freedom enjoyed by our people above all other peoples. But it is difficult to reconcile that boast with a state of the law which, practically, puts the brand of servitude and degradation upon a large class of our fellow citizens, our equals before the law. The thin disguise of "equal" accommodation for passengers in railroad coaches will not mislead any one, nor atone for the wrong this day done.

Above: Supreme Court Justice John Marshall Harlan was a firm defender of African-American rights.

FOR WHITE

FOR COLORED

A little girl leaves a
southern coffee shop
through the "colored"
door.

Chapter 3

BEHIND
THE COLOR LINE

Five-year-old Mary Church was thrilled when her father took her along on a business trip to the North. She smiled proudly as the other train passengers greeted Robert, an important man in their hometown of Memphis, Tennessee. When her father left her to visit the smoking car, she remembered to sit "straight and proper," just as her mother had told her.

Suddenly the conductor was looming over Mary. The angry white man wanted to know what she was doing in the first-class car. When the frightened girl could not answer, he yanked her from her seat. Turning to a white passenger, he asked, "Whose little nigger is this?"

At that moment Robert Church hurried back. The conductor backed down in the face of the angry black man. Confused and unhappy, Mary asked her father what she had done wrong. Why had the conductor tried to force her from the clean train car into one that was shabby and dirty? "He refused to talk about the affair," she later recalled, "and forbade me to do so."

Signs of the Times

Following the Supreme Court's decision in the case of *Plessy* v. *Ferguson*, Jim Crow spread like a plague across the South. State and local governments passed laws introducing segregation into practically every area of public life. Blacks were required to sit in the "colored" sections of trains, streetcars, steamboats, and stagecoaches. They were housed apart from whites in hospitals, mental institutions, prisons, reform schools, and orphanages. They used separate doors, stairways, pay windows, and toilets when working in factories and offices. They were assigned to separate sections of theaters and separate pews at the back of white churches. They were even buried in separate cemeteries. Some towns dug up the bodies of African Americans who had been buried for years and moved them to new locations, where they would not trouble any neighboring white corpses.

The legal restrictions of the Jim Crow system were often spelled out in elaborate detail. Laws might specify the thickness of the barriers required to separate the races in public places or the distance permitted between lines of white and black ticket buyers. One Georgia law prohibited any black amateur baseball team from playing ball "on any vacant lot or baseball diamond within two blocks of any playground devoted to the white race." In Birmingham, Alabama, it was illegal for "a negro and white person to play together or in company with each other in any game of cards or dice, dominoes or checkers."

This run-down store in rural Florida was restricted to black customers by "police order."

In South Carolina, circuses were required to "maintain two main entrances . . . , and such main entrances shall be plainly marked 'For White People,' and the other entrance shall be marked 'For Colored People.'"

The separate facilities provided for blacks were generally smaller, dirtier, and more poorly maintained than those for whites. W. E. B. DuBois, the great black writer and educator who grew up during Reconstruction, described the typical Jim Crow train car as

> half or a quarter or an eighth of the oldest car in service on the road. . . . The plush [seat covering] is caked with dirt, the floor is grimy, and the windows dirty. . . . It is difficult to get lunch or clean water. Lunch rooms either don't serve niggers or

serve them at some dirty and ill-attended hole in the wall. As for toilet rooms,—don't! . . . There is not in the world a more disgraceful denial of human brotherhood than the "Jim-Crow" car of the southern United States.

Sometimes it was impossible or inconvenient to create separate facilities for the races. In those cases African Americans were simply excluded. Blacks were barred from most hotels and restaurants in the South (although eating places might serve them at the back door). They were forbidden to enter most libraries, amusement parks, bowling alleys, and swimming pools, along with many other public and private facilities. Factories and other businesses that could not set up separate work areas for white and black employees found a simple solution: they eliminated black workers altogether.

Jim Crow at School

For African-American children, the most compelling evidence of Jim Crow was often found at school. Most northern schools had long been segregated. That practice became common in the South, too, when the public school system was established there during the Reconstruction era. After the end of Reconstruction, the informal practice of school segregation was written into southern state laws. Florida's education law was typical. It decreed that "the schools for white children and the schools for negro children shall be conducted separately."

As always, *separate* did not mean *equal*. While many white children learned their ABCs in bright, modern, well-equipped classrooms, schools for black children were usually dilapidated

THE RISE OF JIM CROW

A segregated school in Kentucky, around 1916

one-room shacks. The floors were bare, splintery wood. The furniture consisted of crude tables and hard benches made from split logs. The plumbing often leaked. The toilets were often out of order. The textbooks were old and torn. Class sizes were large, with one poorly paid teacher responsible for fifty or more children of varying ages. As a teacher in a North Carolina black school noted, attending classes in a building that resembled "a tobacco barn" did not necessarily rule out a good education. "It does hurt, though, to have the largest classes, the poorest paid teacher, the shortest school year, and an acute shortage of books, paper, pencils, blackboards, and maps."

Behind these deplorable conditions was the racist attitude that educating African Americans was a waste of time and money. White civic leaders argued that black children did not have the same capacity for learning as white children. Furthermore, since blacks could not possibly use their education to get ahead in the world, it was pointless—even dangerous—to fill their heads with "useless" knowledge and ambitions. In a newspaper editorial written in 1899, future Mississippi governor James K. Vardaman said it plainly: "Their education only spoils a good field hand."

Attitudes like this led southern governments to budget far more money for white schools than black schools. South Carolina spent $6.51 a year on each white child in school and $1.55 on each black child. In Mississippi 60 percent of the school-age children were black, but black schools received only 19 percent of the state's education funds. When budgets were tight, funds that had been set aside for black schools went to white schools instead.

Black schools were often closed a few months into the school year, while white schools continued to operate on the money collected from both black and white taxpayers.

Black communities responded to the neglect of their children's education by building and supplying their own schools. Many black southerners donated their labor and their last pennies to help build both public and private schools. At the beginning of the twentieth century, three-quarters of all black high school students in the South attended privately owned and operated schools. Many of the graduates of those schools would go on to become teachers, librarians, doctors, lawyers, journalists, and other community leaders.

Black workers build an extension onto Tuskegee Institute, a famous black college founded in Alabama in 1881.

Ely Green was born in 1893 in a small college town in Tennessee. The light-skinned black boy was eight years old before he learned his first lessons about racism. Ely and two white friends had earned fifteen cents each for raking a neighbor's lawn. When they went to the drugstore to buy soft drinks, the man behind the soda counter served the two white boys, then turned his back. "Where is my drink?" asked Ely.

"You don't get any," said the man. "I don't make drinks for no nigger."

"This was the first time I ever felt hurt, except when my mother died," recalled Ely. Many more hurts and insults would follow. Gradually the little boy would learn that in the Jim Crow world, whites were born to rule and blacks were born to "do what the white man tells them to do." By the time he turned eighteen, Ely had made a solemn vow. He would never bow and scrape before any person, black or white. Instead, he "would be a man in the eyes of man and God."

FIRST ENCOUNTERS

Like young Ely Green, black children in both the North and South never forgot their first encounters with Jim Crow. For Robert Russa Moton of Virginia, it was the time his best friend, a white boy, returned home from boarding school and refused to shake his hand. James Robinson remembered being yanked off the steps of a bus in Tennessee and told to "get the hell back there and wait till the white people get on." Benjamin Elijah Mays of South Carolina watched helplessly one day in 1898 as a group of armed white men cursed his father, forcing him to take off his hat and bow to them. "I was not yet five years old," Mays later wrote, "but I have never forgotten them. . . . That mob is my earliest memory."

As children like these grew up, they would learn hard lessons about the power of white men and women over blacks. Humiliating reminders of their "inferiority" were everywhere: in the places they were forbidden to enter, in the signs that marked everything from restrooms to phone booths to water fountains as "white" and "colored." Albon Holsey, who grew up in Georgia, recalled feeling "beaten" by the time he was fifteen. "I knew that I could only sit in the peanut gallery at our theatre, and could only ride . . . in the Jim Crow car in the train. I had bumped into the color line and knew that so far as white people were concerned, I was just another nigger."

On top of all the legal restrictions, unwritten laws of behavior governed every encounter between the races. A white southerner might call a black man or woman "Boy," "Girl," "Uncle," or "Auntie." In turn, blacks were expected to address white people as "Mister," "Missus," or "Miss." A black man took off his hat and stepped aside when whites passed him on the street. He went to the back door of white homes. He submitted quietly when he was ordered about and insulted.

Even submission was no guarantee against harassment and violence. Blacks who succeeded in business, dressed well, built nice homes, or showed other signs of stepping out of their "place" might be beaten, whipped, or even killed. Some whites harassed blacks simply for amusement. Growing up in rural Georgia, Ed Brown learned to get off the road and hide whenever he heard someone coming. "My motto was, when I was a boy, Don't Meet Nobody. . . . Because nine times out of ten you'd be made to dance, or to drink some whiskey."

THE ART OF SURVIVAL

When it was impossible to avoid encounters with whites, black southerners found other ways to endure. Benjamin Elijah Mays remembered the Jim Crow South as a "perilous world." A black child who "wanted to live a halfway normal life and die a natural death . . . had to learn early the art of how to get along with white folks."

"Getting along" meant carefully avoiding any word, expression, or action that could be interpreted as impertinent or "uppity." It meant coping with humiliation and abuse while somehow holding on to one's dignity and sense of worth. Blacks learned to hide their feelings, intelligence, and achievements under a veil of submission. "I've had to play dumb some-

Two small white children mock a black man on a street corner in 1901.

times," explained Ned Cobb, who grew up in Alabama in the late 1800s. "I knowed not to go too far and let them know what I knowed, because they taken exception of it too quick."

Even as they did what they had to do in order to survive under Jim Crow, many African Americans burned with feelings of rage and frustration. The young men and women born after the end of slavery found it particularly difficult to follow the unwritten laws of the racist system. White southerners regarded these "New Negroes" with alarm. "The generation of

Negroes which have grown up since the war," complained one Memphis newspaper, "have lost in large measure the traditional and wholesome awe of the white race which kept the Negroes in subjection." Some older blacks worried that assertiveness would get their children and grandchildren into trouble. Most African Americans, though, were proud of the younger generation's determination to escape the constant humiliating reminders of white supremacy.

Ned Cobb saw that his sharecropping father "wasn't a slave but he lived like one. Because he had to take what the white people gived to get along." As a young boy, Ned plowed his father's fields and listened to his scoldings. But at age nineteen, he defied his father's warnings and told a white neighbor to keep his cow out of their corn. That small act of defiance made him feel "that I was a man. . . . I wasn't sassy and impudent to nobody, but I done got to the wrong age on me then to feel like it was right for folks to run over me."

Mary Church Terrell helped lead the fight for women's suffrage and civil rights for African Americans.

Black southerners like Ned Cobb would spend much of their lives struggling against the Jim Crow system. Lacking political power and wealth, they could not hope to defeat the overwhelming forces of white supremacy. Still, they refused to bow their heads in resignation. "We have no sympathy with the idea of the 'good old darkey,'" declared a southern black newspaper in 1898. "One generation more, and the Negro that can be kicked, fed on promises, and called by any name, will be gone and a new Negro will come to the front."

Born to wealth, Mary Church enjoyed opportunities that were unusual for a young black woman in the Jim Crow South. After graduating from Oberlin College in Ohio, she traveled and studied in Europe. When she returned to the United States, Mary married Robert Terrell, a lawyer who would become the first black municipal court judge in Washington, D.C.

Mary Church Terrell became a leader in the struggle for equal rights for blacks and women. She and her husband were one of the wealthiest and most respected couples in Washington. When they tried to buy a house, however, they faced the same discrimination as less fortunate African Americans. One real estate agent took their deposit, then returned it. The man "frankly admitted that he could not sell me the house," recalled Mary,

> because the owner had discovered that a colored family wanted it and refused to let us have it. . . . "It is well for you," said the agent, . . . "that you did not succeed in getting that house. If you had, you would have been boycotted by everybody upon whom you would have had to depend for supplies. Neither the milkman nor the iceman would have served you. And every time you or the other members of your family appeared on the street, the boys in the neighborhood would have pelted you with bricks and stones."

An illustration from a French newspaper dramatizes the brutal crime of lynching.

Chapter 4

Ida B. Wells and the Anti-lynching Campaign

John Hughes, South Carolina, 1892: *Hanged for being "saucy to white people."*

Meredith Lewis, Louisiana, 1892: *Lynched after a jury found him innocent of murder.*

Thomas Smith, Virginia, 1893: *Shot to death after arguing with a white businesswoman.*

Lee Walker, Tennessee, 1893: *Burned alive for "attempted assault" after asking two white girls for a ride in their wagon.*

William Brooks, Arkansas, 1894: *Lynched for proposing to a white woman.*

Sam Hose, Georgia, 1899: *Burned alive after killing his white employer in self-defense.*

Daniel Barber, his son and two daughters, Georgia, 1915: *Hanged for illegally selling liquor.*

Mary Turner, Georgia, 1918: *Burned alive for protesting the lynching of her husband. Mary was eight months pregnant.*

Lloyd Clay, Mississippi, 1919: *Burned alive for rape. The rape victim had denied that Clay was her assailant.*

Two young African-American men were lynched in the courthouse square in Marion, Indiana, in 1930.

A REIGN OF TERROR

No one knows the names of all the African Americans lynched in the days of Jim Crow. According to various estimates, some 2,500 to 3,400 blacks may have died at the hands of southern lynch mobs between 1882 and 1930. The worst violence took place in the 1890s. During that bloody decade, blacks were lynched at the rate of one about every two days.

Lynching is a crime in which victims accused of offenses are murdered by lawless mobs. The victims of lynching included whites and blacks, men and women, all across the United States. The vast majority, however, were black men living in small towns and rural communities in the South. Many of the victims were "New Negroes"—members of the younger generation who often refused to act as meek and submissive as their parents.

Southern lynch mobs were typically made up of "respectable" members of the white community. The mobs seized black men and women who had been accused of offenses ranging from "insolence" to petty theft to murder. The victims were dragged to a public place, where a crowd often gathered.

Seventeen-year-old Jesse Washington was mutilated and burned to death in Waco, Texas, in 1916.

Some lynchings were scheduled in advance, so that white children could be excused from school to witness the "festive" occasion. Most lynching victims were hanged or shot. Others were tortured and burned alive. Local political leaders rarely made any attempt to protect the victims. In fact, in many cases, law officers actively participated in lynchings.

The purpose of lynching was not to punish criminals. Instead, the real aim of southern lynch mobs was to terrorize blacks and maintain white supremacy. A black man or woman who challenged Jim Crow in any way, large or small, faced the possibility of torture and murder. As one black southerner observed, the guilt of the victim was unimportant. Lynch mobs performed their savage deeds "knowing full well that one Negro swinging from a tree will serve as well as another to terrorize the community."

TELLING THE WORLD

In 1892 three young black men opened a grocery store in a black suburb of Memphis, Tennessee. Thomas Moss and his

A BRUTAL WARNING

After a lynching the members of the mob often posed proudly to have their pictures taken. Photographers used portable printing presses to issue postcards showing the lynching victim surrounded by the cheerful crowd. One postcard issued in 1908 featured a photo of five black men dangling from a tree, along with this poem as a caption:

This is only the branch of a Dogwood tree;
An emblem of WHITE SUPREMACY.
A lesson once taught in the Pioneer's school,
That this is a land of WHITE MAN'S RULE.
The Red Man once in an early day,
Was told by the Whites to mend his way.

The negro, now, by eternal grace,
Must learn to stay in the negro's place.
In the Sunny South, the Land of the Free,
Let the WHITE SUPREME forever be.
Let this a warning to all negroes be,
Or they'll suffer the fate of
    the DOGWOOD TREE.

two partners worked hard to build a thriving business. Their success angered the white owner of the area's only other grocery store. When the white man sent armed thugs to wipe out the competition, Moss and his friends fought back, wounding several of the vandals. The three black storekeepers were arrested. A few days later, a lynch mob dragged them from jail, lined them up, and shot them dead.

News of the lynching shocked Ida B. Wells. The thirty-year-old black journalist had been a good friend of Thomas Moss and his family. As editor of the black Memphis newspaper *Free Speech*, Wells had often stood up against racism and segregation. In 1884, after being ejected from a whites-only train car, she had challenged Tennessee's Separate Car Law. Wells had won a lawsuit against the railroad and a victory against Jim Crow (although the verdict was later overturned by a higher court). Now the crusading journalist resolved to use the power of the press to expose the brutal racism behind the murders of Thomas Moss and his partners.

Wells began her campaign with a thorough investigation of lynching cases. Southern whites often excused the crime by claiming that lynch mobs were needed to protect virtuous white women from brutal black rapists. In fact, Wells found, fewer than one-third of all lynching victims were accused of rape, and in most such cases there was evidence that the accusations were false. "Nobody in this section of the country believes the old threadbare lie that Negro men rape white women," wrote the journalist. Instead, the myth of black rapists was just "an excuse to get rid of Negroes who were acquiring wealth and property and thus keep the race terrorized and 'keep the nigger down.'"

Those conclusions outraged the white citizens of Memphis. After an angry mob destroyed her printing presses, Wells was forced to flee the South. She continued her relentless campaign against lynching, however, writing articles and books and giving lectures throughout the Northeast. The courageous young activist even traveled to Great Britain to "tell the world the facts."

Ida B. Wells's efforts rallied countless supporters to the anti-lynching cause. Other black leaders and organizations joined the war on lynching, campaigning for federal intervention against the crime. While their efforts raised public awareness about lynching, they never succeeded in persuading Congress to pass a federal anti-lynching law. While the number of

Women's rights advocate and anti-lynching crusader Ida B. Wells

A New Orleans newspaper announces the scheduled lynching of a Mississippi black man in June 1919.

lynchings slowly declined after the 1890s, the brutal practice would not completely die out until the early 1960s.

A farmworker accused of assaulting a white woman in Sherman, Texas, is taken to court in chains.

JIM CROW IN COURT

"Negroes always got the worst of it," recalled Benjamin Mays of South Carolina. "Guilt and innocence were meaningless words. . . . Whenever a white man was involved, the Negro was automatically guilty."

For African Americans accused of crime, the sort of "justice" handed down by southern courts was often little better than the brutality of the lynch mob. Under the Jim Crow system, blacks were not permitted to serve on juries. They were often denied the right to testify in court and to be represented by a competent lawyer. They were tried before white judges and juries, who based their verdicts not on the evidence but on the assumption that blacks were naturally more "primitive" and immoral than whites.

Black defendants were punished harshly for even minor offenses. Meanwhile, whites accused of the same crimes were excused or given light sentences. Whites accused of crimes against blacks were almost never punished. One black song summed it up this way:

> If a white man kills a negro, they hardly carry it
>   to court,
> If a negro kills a white man, they hang him like
>   a goat.

The unequal justice system not only helped enforce white supremacy but also enriched southern state treasuries. Under a system known as "convict leasing," tens of thousands of black men and women were sentenced to long terms at hard labor, often for minor offenses such as gambling or vagrancy. The convicts were leased to plantation owners, factory owners, mine operators, railroads, and other private employers. The states collected fees from the employers. The employers enjoyed a steady supply of cheap labor. Everyone benefited except for the convicts unjustly sentenced to a life that was often worse than slavery.

Black convicts perform hard labor in a rock quarry near their prison.

Convict laborers worked fourteen or more hours each day. Bound in heavy chains, they labored in fields, mines, and factories under the watchful eye of guards who were quick to punish any signs of "slacking." The convicts slept in open stockades. Their meals were few and meager. The harsh treatment and dangerous working conditions contributed to high rates of sickness, injury, and death. Inspectors visiting a prison hospital in Jackson, Mississippi, in 1887 found

> twenty-six inmates, all of whom have been lately brought there off the farms and railroads, . . . all bearing on their persons marks of the most inhuman and brutal treatment. Most of them have their backs cut in great wales [welts], scars and blisters, some with the skin peeling off in pieces as the result of severe

beatings. . . . They are lying there dying, some of them on bare boards, so poor and emaciated [starved] that their bones almost come through their skin.

In the early twentieth century, investigations by newspapers, labor unions, and government agencies uncovered the horrendous abuses in convict leasing. The system was gradually abolished. In its place, African Americans were sent to prisons or county chain gangs, where conditions were usually no better. Reflecting on the state of southern law and justice, one black man from South Carolina concluded, "De courts [of] dis land is not for niggers. . . . When it come to trouble, de law an' a nigger is de white man's sport, an' justice is a stranger in them precincts, an' mercy is unknown."

URBAN RACE WARS

Around the turn of the twentieth century, racial violence rocked cities in both the North and South. Between 1898 and 1908, the list of cities torn by violence included Wilmington, North Carolina; Washington, D.C.; New York City; Akron, Ohio; New Orleans, Louisiana; Springfield, Ohio; Atlanta, Georgia; Brownsville, Texas; Greensburg, Indiana; and Springfield, Illinois. Newspapers called the disturbances "race riots." In reality, these "riots" were massacres of African Americans by white mobs.

The Atlanta riot of September 1906 was sparked by a series of inflammatory newspaper articles. For months local papers had been reporting on trivial encounters between black men and white women, inflating them into "an intolerable epidemic of rape." On September 22 news of another "rape" sent an angry white mob swarming into the black section of the city. The rioters, who included members of Atlanta's most prominent families, attacked every black man, woman, and child in sight. Victims were chased down, dragged from streetcars, beaten, clubbed, shot, and mutilated. Twenty-five African Americans were killed and hundreds were injured in the four-day rampage. Countless black homes and businesses were looted and burned.

White children cheer after setting a black family's home on fire during a Chicago race riot in 1919.

The most serious northern riot took place in Springfield, the capital of Illinois. In August 1908 a white woman accused a black man of assaulting her. When the woman admitted that the charges were false, the man was released from prison. That infuriated Springfield's white citizens. Thousands took to the streets, shouting, "Lincoln freed you, we'll show you where you belong." By the time the state militia restored order three days later, ten blacks had been lynched, more than seventy had been injured, and many black homes and businesses had been destroyed.

The entire nation was stunned by this outburst of racial violence in a northern capital. Journalist William English Walling went to Springfield to investigate. Walling found that many of the rioters' victims were middle-class blacks who had managed to get an education and build a successful career or business. The true cause of the Springfield riot, he concluded, was not anger over black crime but fear and resentment of black achievement. "A large part of the white population," Walling wrote, was engaged in "permanent warfare with the Negro race."

Booker T. Washington was the most widely respected and influential black leader of the Jim Crow era.

Chapter 5

THE AGE OF ACCOMMODATION

BOOKER T. WASHINGTON'S EARLIEST MEMORIES were of the slave quarters. Born on a Virginia plantation in 1856, Booker lived in a crude log cabin with his brother, sister, and his mother, an enslaved cook. He never knew the name of his white father.

At the end of the Civil War, Booker's family moved to West Virginia. There the young boy helped support his struggling family by working in the coal mines and a salt-packing plant. Years later, he would recall that he always felt "an intense longing to learn to read." With the help of an old spelling book, he taught himself the alphabet. When the first school for blacks opened in the area, he worked before dawn and in the evenings so that he could attend daytime classes. Then, one day, the ambitious boy learned about a new school in Virginia where poor black students could work to pay their way. From that point on, he was "on fire constantly with one ambition, and that was to go to Hampton."

At age sixteen, Booker fulfilled his dream. Setting out with just a few dollars in his pocket, he traveled five hundred miles, hitching wagon rides and walking part of the way. At last he arrived in what seemed like the "promised land." Booker was accepted into the Hampton Institute. He studied there for three years, paying for his lodging and tuition by working as the school janitor. After graduation he stayed on at Hampton to teach and continue his studies.

In 1881 Booker T. Washington was hired as the first principal of a new school opening in Tuskegee, Alabama. Arriving in the small town, he found no school buildings or equipment—only "hundreds of hungry, earnest souls who wanted to secure knowledge." Within a few years, he would transform the Tuskegee Institute into one of the best-known black schools in the country.

Tuskegee offered a program known as "industrial education." (Today we might call it "vocational training.") The students built their own classrooms. They raised and cooked their own food. They learned practical skills such as carpentry, shoemaking, blacksmithing, and improved methods of farming. Washington's goal was to give young men and women "a practical knowledge of some one industry, together with the spirit of industry, thrift, and economy," so that they could make a living in the kinds of jobs open to blacks in the South. He firmly believed that African Americans could overcome white hostility and prejudice "through [their] skill, intelligence, and character." The future of the black man, Washington would later say,

> rested largely upon the question as to whether or not
> he [could] make himself . . . of such undeniable

Students learn the trade of cabinetmaking in a workshop at Tuskegee Institute.

value to the community in which he lived that the community could not dispense with his presence. . . . Any individual who learned to do something better than anybody else . . . had solved his problem, regardless of the colour of his skin.

THE ATLANTA COMPROMISE

In 1895 Booker T. Washington was invited to speak at the Cotton States and International Exposition in Atlanta, Georgia. It would be the first time a black person had ever addressed a national convention of white leaders in the South. The former slave was nervous. He worked hard to prepare a speech that he hoped would "cement the friendship of the races and bring about hearty cooperation between them." When he stepped onstage, the mostly white audience greeted him with scattered applause. When he finished speaking, the hall exploded in "an uproar of enthusiasm."

Washington began the speech that would become known as the Atlanta Compromise by urging African Americans to stop striving for immediate racial equality. Instead, they should try to improve themselves through education and honest labor. Progress in voting rights and other "privileges of the law" would come gradually, as they "prepared [themselves] for the exercise of these privileges." Washington told his white audience that blacks were willing to accept segregation in return for economic opportunities. He assured them that supporting black education and economic advancement would benefit the entire South. "In all things that are purely social we can be as separate as the fingers," he declared, "yet one as the hand in all things essential to mutual progress."

The Atlanta Compromise speech made Booker T. Washington a national celebrity. Both southern and northern whites applauded his policy of compromise, or "accommodation." They believed that "accommodationism" would promote economic development in the South by producing a permanent underclass of contented, well-trained, industrious black workers. Millions of African Americans also looked up to the famous educator. It was hard not to admire someone who had risen from slavery to the heights of success.

From 1895 to his death in 1915, Booker T. Washington was regarded as the chief spokesperson for black America. Government leaders consulted him on questions involving the African-American community. Southern civic leaders asked his advice before appointing black teachers and principals. Wealthy white northerners donated large sums of money to Tuskegee and dozens of similar "industrial schools" founded throughout the South.

Evidence of the black educator's renown came in 1901, when he became the first African American invited to dine at the White House. White southerners condemned President Theodore Roosevelt for what one editor called the violation of "our long-matured views on the subject of social intercourse between blacks and whites." A black newspaper responded by mocking whites for being "shocked, boiled, smitten, and exasperated" just because the president had shared a meal "with a coloured gentleman who had been entertained by the nobility of England, and the best people of America."

Booker T. Washington's dinner with President Theodore Roosevelt is portrayed as a victory in the struggle for racial equality.

W. E. B. DuBois Speaks Out

Among the many tributes Booker T. Washington received after his Atlanta Compromise speech was a short note congratulating him on his "phenomenal success." That note came from the man who would soon become one of his most vocal critics: William Edward Burghardt DuBois.

W. E. B. DuBois's background was very different from Booker Washington's. Unlike the former slave, DuBois had been born and raised in freedom in the North. He had received scholarships to some of the world's finest schools, including Fisk University in Nashville, Tennessee, and Harvard University. The gifted young man had become the first African American to obtain a doctorate (an advanced degree) from Harvard.

While studying in Tennessee, DuBois had spent his summers teaching at black country schools. For the first time, he had come face to face with the terrible poverty, prejudice, and

Civil rights activist W. E. B. DuBois became the leading opponent of accommodationism.

THE TORCH PASSES

In February 1895 America mourned the passing of Frederick Douglass. Born into slavery, Douglass had escaped to freedom and become a leader in the abolitionist cause. For more than half a century, he had inspired audiences with his stirring speeches and writings on the horrors of the slave system. During Reconstruction, Douglass had fought for laws guaranteeing African Americans the rights of citizenship. In his final years, he had watched in frustration as southern whites trampled his people's hard-won rights and freedoms. "There is no Negro problem," Douglass had roared in one of his last major addresses. "The problem is whether the American people have honesty enough, loyalty enough, honor enough, patriotism enough to live up to their own Constitution."

A few months after Frederick Douglass's death, Booker T. Washington gave his famous Atlanta Compromise speech. Almost overnight Washington was acclaimed as the next great black leader. Not everyone was pleased with that development. Douglass had been a fearless, relentless champion of racial equality. To some African Americans, it seemed wrong for his torch of leadership to pass to a man willing to "compromise" with injustice.

Above: Frederick Douglass dedicated his life to the fight for African-American freedom and racial equality.

discrimination endured by southern blacks. His experiences left him with a strong commitment to the advancement of his race. Like Washington, DuBois believed that education and industry were the keys to African-American progress. He agreed that vocational training was important, although he also believed in higher education for the most talented black men and women. He was even willing to accept limitations on voting rights for the "good many of our people" who were not yet "fit for the responsibility of republican government."

Over time, however, DuBois grew increasingly critical of Booker Washington's policies. In the years following the Atlanta Compromise, most blacks had tried the accommodationist approach, but conditions had only gotten worse in the South. DuBois was also concerned that the "Tuskegee machine" Washington's powerful network of supporters— had become too powerful. Partly because of the influence of the Tuskegee machine, African Americans were finding it harder than ever to attain higher education and to speak out for their civil and political rights. "Things came to such a pass," DuBois later reflected, "that when any Negro complained or advocated a course of action, he was silenced with the remark that Mr. Washington did not agree with this."

In 1903 W. E. B. DuBois made a complete break with Booker T. Washington. In a collection of essays titled *The Souls of Black Folk*, he attacked the black leader's policy of "adjustment and submission." He denounced Washington's opposition to higher education, pointing out that the industrial schools could not operate without the teachers trained in black colleges. Most of all, DuBois criticized Washington for accepting "the alleged inferiority of the Negro races" and asking African Americans to give up their essential rights. "So far as Mr. Washington apologizes for injustice, North or South," wrote DuBois,

> [and] does not rightly value the privilege and duty of voting, . . . and opposes the higher training and ambition of our brighter minds—so far as he, the South, or the nation, does this—we must unceasingly and firmly oppose them. By every civilized and peaceful method we must strive for the rights which the world accords to men.

THE BIRTH OF THE NAACP

W. E. B. DuBois was not alone in his condemnation of Booker T. Washington's accommodationist policies. A small but vocal group of young black intellectuals had also begun to speak out against the Atlanta Compromise. In 1905 DuBois invited twenty-eight of these young radicals to a conference at Niagara Falls.

For three days the members of the "Niagara Movement" debated a long list of grievances and demands. Then they issued a Declaration of Principles. On behalf of all African Americans, they protested racism and discrimination. They demanded full political and civil rights, equal treatment before the law, and equal opportunities in education and employment. They also pledged to

> complain, and to complain loudly and insistently. To ignore, overlook, or apologize for these wrongs is to prove ourselves unworthy of freedom. Persistent manly agitation is the way to liberty, and toward this goal the Niagara Movement has started and asks the cooperation of all men of all races.

The Niagara Movement's brand of fiery protest was too radical for most African Americans. From the beginning, the group struggled to attract members and raise funds. By 1908, it was nearly bankrupt. But its ideas lived on, lighting the way to the formation of a new and more successful organization.

After the 1908 race riot in Springfield, Illinois, many northern white reformers had taken a hard look at the racial injustice in their own backyard. Social worker Mary White Ovington and journalist William English Walling decided that it was time to form an organization that would fight for an end to discrimination throughout the United States. They issued a summons for civil rights activists to attend a national conference in New York City. Among those who answered the call were W. E. B. DuBois and the other young radicals of the Niagara Movement. In February 1909 the delegates to the conference founded the National Association for the Advancement of Colored People (NAACP).

The NAACP was the first major interracial civil rights group. Within a decade it would grow to include more than 40,000 members, organized in 165 local branches in both the North and South. One of the first issues of the NAACP's monthly magazine, *The Crisis*, made it clear that the organization rejected Booker T. Washington's accommodationist policies. "To treat evil as though it were good and good as though it were evil," wrote the magazine's editor, W. E. B. DuBois, "is not only wrong but dangerous." Instead, blacks and whites who believed in racial equality would work together to "fight the wrong of race prejudice . . . with every human weapon in every civilized way."

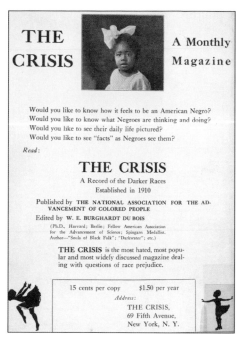

An advertisement for *The Crisis*, the NAACP journal first published in November 1910

BENNIE'S GROCERY
802
West Gwinnett St.
LARD
4 Lbs 35¢
Salt
SYRUP
49 Qt 15¢
Neck BONES
2 Lbs 15¢
RIBS
10¢
GRITS
5 Lbs 10¢
MEAL
CONTAINS LEAD
Grade
GAS
5
Gallons
85¢

The Far Horizon

IN 1913 AFRICAN AMERICANS OBSERVED THE Jubilee—the fiftieth anniversary of the Emancipation Proclamation. Festivals and exhibitions celebrated the progress made by southern blacks since the historic proclamation outlawing slavery in the Confederate states. Illiteracy had fallen from more than 90 percent in 1865 to around 30 percent. More than 500,000 black southerners owned their own homes. About one-quarter of black farmers owned the land they worked. Tens of thousands of southern blacks, including former slaves and their children, had become business owners, doctors, lawyers, and teachers.

As impressive as the advances were, they represented only a fraction of the more than eight million African Americans living in the South. The great majority of those people lived in poverty. Most were poor farmers who labored from sunrise to sunset in the fields of white landowners. Racism was still

Opposite: A black-owned grocery store in the early 1920s

BOOKER T. WASHINGTON'S PRIVATE VIEW

Even Booker T. Washington may have become discouraged by the continuing deterioration of conditions in the South. Washington devoted his life to encouraging "accommodationism." He believed that his approach was the only practical way African Americans could get ahead in the South. At the same time, the powerful black leader secretly helped finance legal challenges to the Jim Crow laws. He wrote anonymous newspaper articles protesting the violation of black civil rights. And in an essay published shortly after his death in 1915, he denounced segregation as "unjust" and "illegal." To the average black man, Washington wrote, segregation

> means that he will receive inferior [housing] in return for the taxes he
> pays . . . that the sewerage in his part of the city will be inferior; that
> the streets and sidewalks will be neglected, that the street lighting will
> be poor; that his section of the city will not be kept in order by the
> police and other authorities, . . . making it difficult for him to rear his
> family in decency. . . .
>
> Practically every thoughtful negro resents [this] injustice. . . . That
> the negro does not express this constant sense of wrong is no proof
> that he does not feel it.

Above: Booker T. Washington on the campus of Tuskegee Institute in 1906

deeply rooted in every aspect of southern life.

While conditions were somewhat better in the North and West, blacks in those areas also found their freedoms and opportunities limited by prejudice and discrimination. In fact, racist attitudes went all the way to the top of American government and society. In 1912 Woodrow Wilson had been elected president after pledging that he wanted to see "justice done to the colored people in every way." One of the new president's first actions was to segregate the work areas, lunchrooms, and restrooms in federal offices in Washington, D.C.

FIGHTING BACK

While black southerners were forced to endure Jim Crow, that did not mean they accepted the system as right or permanent. Instead, many blacks found ways to fight back. Their struggles took the forms of both organized action and quiet resistance.

Abolitionist leader Harriet Tubman was nearly eighty years old when she helped found the National Association of Colored Women.

One of the leaders of the struggle against Jim Crow was the NAACP. The organization sent hundreds of lawyers into courts to challenge discriminatory laws. Its legal team won a number of important cases involving voting rights and segregation in housing and public transportation. NAACP lawyers also defended African Americans unjustly accused of crimes. In addition, the organization waged a forceful campaign against lynching and fought for better police protection for southern blacks.

Several other protest organizations joined the battle for African-American rights. One of the most prominent was the National Association of Colored Women (NACW). The NACW was founded in 1896 by

The NAACP stages a protest against lynching outside the Capitol in Washington, D.C.

a group of black women activists including Ida B. Wells, abolitionists Josephine Ruffin and Harriet Tubman, and Mary Church Terrell. (We met Mary as a young girl in chapter 3, page 33.) The organization was active in campaigns against Jim Crow and lynching and in support of women's suffrage (voting rights). African Americans also formed a number of workers' unions and alliances. In many cases these groups were founded after black workers were excluded from white unions. Black unions staged several strikes in the 1890s, seeking better wages and working conditions.

Thousands of black southerners who never joined a protest group or union supported the fight against Jim Crow by taking part in boycotts. Between 1890 and 1906, African Americans in more than twenty-five southern cities staged boycotts of segregated streetcars. Men, women, and children walked or rode horse-drawn wagons and carriages to work and school to protest the inferior "colored" accommodations. Most of the boycotts lasted just a few days or weeks. Although these protests inspired and united black communities, they rarely resulted in any changes in segregation policies. It would be nearly half a century before African Americans had the economic power and large-scale organization needed to wage a successful battle against the powerful forces of white supremacy.

PILLARS OF THE BLACK COMMUNITY

In the years following Reconstruction, African Americans built strong communities that helped them lead more rewarding lives, even under the shadow of Jim Crow. One of the oldest and most important black institutions was the church. Free northern blacks had developed independent congregations as early as the eighteenth century, and southern blacks had built their own churches during Reconstruction. In the Jim Crow era, these churches became more than simply houses of worship. They were also centers of strength, hope, and refuge.

Blacks in many communities gathered at church to socialize, share information, and discuss important events and issues. Churches also served as social service agencies, providing aid for the unemployed and needy. They sponsored fund-raising drives for schools, orphanages, and homes for the elderly. They offered lectures, concerts, and classes in typing, cooking, and other job skills. Many black churches doubled as boys' and girls' clubs and nurseries for the children of working mothers. Most of the day-to-day work of managing all these activities was performed by black women volunteers.

Toward the end of the nineteenth century, black women also began to form their own clubs to provide aid to the disadvantaged and to work for reforms such as women's suffrage and temperance (the campaign against liquor). Meanwhile, black men joined together in fraternal orders and mutual benefit associations. These organizations offered a variety of benefits, including recreational activities and health and life insurance. In addition, African Americans in many cities formed literary societies, academic societies, charities, and business leagues. Membership in these groups gave men and women a chance to improve themselves, help their neighbors, and practice their leadership skills.

The turn of the century saw a significant rise in the number

A prosperous black-owned pharmacy in Chattanooga, Tennessee, around 1907

of black businesses in the South. Many of these new enterprises catered mainly to African-American customers. White-owned banks, insurance companies, pharmacies, funeral homes, and other businesses often treated black customers with contempt or even refused to serve them. By patronizing black-owned businesses, African Americans supported their communities, and they could be certain they would be treated with respect and appreciation.

Black writers and editors founded newspapers in nearly every major American city during the Jim Crow era. Black newspapers protested discrimination and supported the struggle for civil and political rights. Through the spread of information and ideas, they helped educate and unify the black community.

Schools were another pillar of the black community. African Americans sacrificed to send their children to school and to support the creation of private high schools and colleges. They believed, as one former slave told her granddaughter, that education would give the younger generation a chance "to have a good life and to become something worthwhile."

Schoolteachers, newspaper editors, and business owners were all part of the emerging black middle class, a group that

A middle-class black couple welcomes friends to a backyard barbeque in Lincoln, Nebraska.

also included doctors, lawyers, ministers, postal workers, and railroad porters. The men and women of the black middle class represented the most educated and prosperous members of the African-American community. Despite their success, they still shared the indignities of racial prejudice and segregation. They were restricted to the "colored" sections of trains and street-cars. They were excluded from better city neighborhoods. Their homes and businesses were often targeted by lynch mobs aiming to teach "uppity" blacks their proper "place." After the Atlanta riot of 1906, one of the city's most respected black physicians addressed a group of prominent white citizens. "How shall we protect our lives and property?" asked Dr. W. F. Penn. "If living a sober, industrious, upright life, accumulating property and educating his children as best he knows how, is not the standard by which a coloured man can live and be pro-tected in the South, what is to become of him?"

LOOKING BEYOND

Courage! Look out, beyond, and see
The far horizon's beckoning span!

Faith in your God-known destiny!
We are a part of some great plan.
—from James Weldon Johnson, "Fifty Years"

On January 1, 1913, the *New York Times* published a poem composed by James Weldon Johnson in honor of the year of Jubilee. In "Fifty Years," the poet applauded the strides made by his fellow African Americans in the half century since emancipation. He acknowledged the "staggering force of brutish might" that bowed their spirits until they nearly gave up in despair. He concluded by urging black Americans to continue their fight for full equality in the land that was theirs "by right of birth" and "by right of toil."*

African Americans faced many challenges as they moved forward into the next half century. Racism remained in full force throughout the nation. Imposing obstacles blocked their path to educational, economic, political, and social advancement. Racial violence was on the upsurge, as white terrorist groups revived in the South.

But even in these stormy times, there were signs of hope. Strong black communities had promoted the growth of schools, churches, businesses, newspapers, and social and professional organizations. Those institutions had produced a generation of young black activists who would play a leading role in the struggle against Jim Crow. In the coming decades, many courageous African Americans would answer James Weldon Johnson's challenge. Standing "erect and without fear," they would march toward the far horizon and claim their rightful heritage as American citizens.

* For more on James Weldon Johnson and other great African-American writers, artists, and musicians of the early twentieth century, see volume 6 in this series, *The Harlem Renaissance.*

Glossary

abolitionist A person who works for the abolition, or ending, of slavery.

accommodation The act of compromising with, or adapting to, an opposing point of view. *Accommodationism* often refers to the policy in which blacks adapt to the attitudes and expectations of whites.

Black Codes Laws passed by state and local governments in the South during Reconstruction to restrict the rights and freedoms of former slaves.

Confederate Belonging to the southern states that seceded (withdrew) from the Union during the Civil War, forming a new republic.

disenfranchising Taking away the right to vote.

emancipation Freeing someone from the control or power of another.

homesteader A farmer who acquired ownership of government land under the Homestead Act of 1862.

loam Rich, crumbly soil.

lynching The killing of a person by a lawless mob.

Reconstruction The period from 1865 to 1877, during which the former Confederate states were placed under military rule before being readmitted to the Union.

segregation The practice of separating one race from another by setting up separate housing, schools, and public facilities and through other forms of discrimination.

sharecropper A tenant farmer who lives on and works a plot of land owned by someone else, paying rent by giving the landowner a share of the crops raised.

suffrage The right to vote.

vagrancy The state of being a vagrant, a person without a home or regular work.

To Find Out More

BOOKS

Bair, Barbara. *Though Justice Sleeps: African Americans, 1880-1900.* New York: Oxford University Press, 1997.

Collier, Christopher, and James Lincoln Collier. *Reconstruction and the Rise of Jim Crow, 1864-1896.* New York: Marshall Cavendish, 2000.

George, Charles. *Life under the Jim Crow Laws.* San Diego, CA: Lucent Books, 2000.

Golay, Michael. *Reconstruction and Reaction: The Emancipation of Slaves,*

1861-1913. New York: Facts on File, 1996.

Haskins, Jim. *The Geography of Hope: Black Exodus from the South after Reconstruction.* Brookfield, CT: Twenty-First Century Books, 1999.

Hauser, Pierre. *The Community Builders, 1877-1895: From the End of Reconstruction to the Atlanta Compromise.* New York: Chelsea House, 1996.

WEB SITES

Jim Crow Laws. Spartacus Educational.
http://www.spartacus.schoolnet.co.uk/USAjimcrow.htm

Remembering Jim Crow. American Public Media.
http://americanradioworks.publicradio.org/features/remembering/

The Rise and Fall of Jim Crow. Educational Broadcasting Corporation.
http://www.pbs.org/wnet/jimcrow

Separate Is Not Equal. Smithsonian National Museum of American History.
http://americanhistory.si.edu/brown/history/1-segregated/segregated-america.html

Selected Bibliography

Du Bois, W. E. B. *Writings.* New York: Literary Classics of the United States, 1986.

Fireside, Harvey. *Separate and Unequal: Homer Plessy and the Supreme Court Decision That Legalized Racism.* New York: Carroll and Graf, 2004.

Franklin, John Hope, and Alfred A. Moss Jr. *From Slavery to Freedom: A History of African Americans.* New York: Alfred A. Knopf, 2000.

Green, Ely. *Ely: An Autobiography.* New York: Seabury Press, 1966.

Katz, William Loren. *The Black West: A Documentary and Pictorial History.* Garden City, NY: Doubleday, 1973.

Lewis, David Levering, ed. *W. E. B. Du Bois: A Reader.* New York: Henry Holt, 1995.

Litwack, Leon F. *Trouble in Mind: Black Southerners in the Age of Jim Crow.* New York: Alfred A. Knopf, 1998.

Medley, Keith Weldon. *We As Freemen: Plessy v. Ferguson.* Gretna, LA: Pelican Publishing, 2003.

Packard, Jerrold M. *American Nightmare: The History of Jim Crow.* New York: St. Martin's, 2002.

Painter, Nell Irvin. *Exodusters: Black Migrations to Kansas after Reconstruction.* New York: Alfred A. Knopf, 1977.

Rubel, David. *The Coming Free: The Struggle for African-American Equality.*

New York: DK Publishing, 2005.

Terrell, Mary Church. *A Colored Woman in a White World.* Amherst, NY: Humanity Books, 2005.

Washington, Booker T. *Up from Slavery.* New York: New American Library, 2000.

Weinstein, Allen, and Frank Otto Gatell. *The Segregation Era, 1863-1954: A Modern Reader.* New York: Oxford University Press, 1970.

Wells-Barnett, Ida B. *On Lynchings.* Amherst, NY: Humanity Books, 2002.

Woodward, C. Vann. *The Strange Career of Jim Crow: A Commemorative Edition.* New York: Oxford University Press, 2002.

Notes on Quotes

Introduction

p. 09, "The slave went free": Du Bois, *Black Reconstruction in America,* p. 30.

Chapter 1: The Exodusters

p. 11, "The man I rented": Painter, *Exodusters,* p. 3.

p. 12, "rights and interests": C. Vann Woodward, "The Danger of Retreating from the Second Reconstruction," *Southern Changes* 4, no. 1 (1981): p. 14.

p. 12, "The whole South": ibid., p. 133.

p. 13, "Our old masters": Painter, *Exodusters,* p. 67.

p. 14, "their little store": Litwack, *Trouble in Mind,* p. 484.

p. 14, "If you try": Painter, *Exodusters,* p. 3.

p. 15, "To the Colored Citizens": Katz, *The Black West,* p. 168.

p. 16, "the rebel-ridden South": Haskins, *The Geography of Hope,* p. 90.

p. 16, "long pent-up hatred": Painter, *Exodusters,* p. 184.

p. 18, "nearly half a thousand": ibid., p. 198.

p. 18, "I looked on the ground": ibid., p. 4.

Chapter 2: The Birth of Jim Crow

p. 24, "Come listen all you": "Jump Jim Crow" at http://www.edu-cyberpg.com/Music/statesong.html

p. 26, "now the policy" and "No Republican leader": Woodward, *The Strange Career of Jim Crow,* p. 73.

p. 26, "on account of race": "15th Amendment to the Constitution" at http://www.loc.gov/rr/program/bib/ourdocs/15thamendment.html

p. 28, "asks no special favors": "Defense of the Negro Race, Speech of Hon. George H. White, of North Carolina, in the House of Representatives, Jan-

uary 29, 1901," at http://docsouth.unc.edu/nc/whitegh/whitegh.html

p. 29, "The law . . . which prohibits": Medley, *We As Freemen,* pp. 99-100.

p. 29, "I am a colored man": Fireside, *Separate and Unequal,* p. 1.

p. 29, "real object" and "to keep Negroes": ibid., p. 195.

p. 30, "the enforced separation": ibid., pp. 342-343.

p. 31, "In view of": Medley, *We As Freemen,* pp. 204-205.

Chapter 3: Behind the Color Line

p. 33, "straight and proper": Terrell, *A Colored Woman in a White World,* p. 46.

p. 34, "on any vacant": " 'Jim Crow' Laws" at
    http://www.nps.gov/archive/malu/documents/jim_crow_laws.htm

p. 34, "a negro and white person": "Separate Is Not Equal" at http://american-
    history.si.edu/brown/history/1-segregated/detail/jim-crow-laws.html

p. 35, "maintain two main entrances": Packard, *American Nightmare,* p. 93.

p. 35, "half or a quarter": W. E. B. Du Bois, *Darkwater: Voices from within the
    Veil,* at http://www.web-books.com/Classics/AuthorsAD/DuBois/Dark-
    water/DuBois_DarkwaterC11P2.htm

p. 36, "the schools for white": "'Jim Crow' Laws" at
    http://www.nps.gov/archive/malu/documents/jim_crow_laws.htm

p. 37, "a tobacco barn": Litwack, *Trouble in Mind,* p. 106.

p. 38, "Their education": George, *Life under the Jim Crow Laws,* pp. 37-38.

p. 39, "Where is my drink": Green, *Ely,* p. 13.

p. 39, "do what the white": ibid., p. 31.

p. 39, "would be a man": ibid., p. 89.

p. 39, "get the hell": Litwack, *Trouble in Mind,* p. 10.

p. 39, "I was not yet": ibid., pp. 12-13.

p. 40, "I knew that I": ibid., p. 16.

p. 40, "My motto was": ibid., p. 10.

p. 41, "perilous world": ibid., p. 7.

p. 41, "I've had to play": ibid., p. 413.

p. 41, "The generation of Negroes": ibid., p. 198.

p. 42, "wasn't a slave": ibid., p. 50.

p. 42, "We have no sympathy": ibid., p. 417.

p. 43, "frankly admitted": Terrell, *A Colored Woman in a White World,* p. 153.

Chapter 4: Ida B. Wells and the Anti-lynching Campaign

p. 45, "saucy to white people": Wells-Barnett, *On Lynchings,* p. 95.

p. 47, "knowing full well": Litwack, *Trouble in Mind,* p. 290.

p. 48, "This is only the branch": ibid., p. 287.

p. 49, "Nobody in this section": Rubel, *The Coming Free,* p. 19.

p. 49, "an excuse": Packard, *American Nightmare,* p. 139.

p. 49, "tell the world": Wells-Barnett, *On Lynchings,* p. 151.

p. 50, "Negroes always got": Litwack, *Trouble in Mind,* p. 247.

p. 50, "If a white man": ibid., p. 253.

p. 51, "twenty-six inmates": "The History of Jim Crow" at http://www.jim-crowhistory.org/history/creating2.htm

p. 52, "De courts": Litwack, *Trouble in Mind,* p. 276.

p. 52, "an intolerable epidemic": Weinstein and Gatell, *The Segregation Era,* p. 115.

p. 53, "Lincoln freed you": Rubel, *The Coming Free,* p. 24.

p. 53, "A large part": William Walling, "The Race War in the North," *The Independent,* September 3, 1908, at http://www.spartacus.schoolnet.co.uk/USAwalling.htm

Chapter 5: The Age of Accommodation

p. 55, "an intense longing": Washington, *Up from Slavery,* p. 19.

p. 55, "on fire constantly": ibid., p. 29.

p. 56, "promised land": ibid., p. 35.

p. 56, "hundreds of hungry": ibid., p. 75.

p. 56, "a practical knowledge": ibid., p. 88.

p. 56, "through [their] skill" and "rested largely": ibid., p. 141.

p. 57, "cement the friendship": ibid., p. 151.

p. 57, "an uproar of enthusiasm": Hauser, *The Community Builders,* p. 141.

p. 58, "privileges of the law": Washington, *Up from Slavery,* p. 155.

p. 58, "In all things": ibid., p. 154.

p. 59, "our long-matured" and "shocked, boiled": Franklin and Moss, *From Slavery to Freedom,* p. 341.

p. 59, "phenomenal success": Bair, *Though Justice Sleeps,* p. 99.

p. 60, "There is no Negro problem": "Images from the 1893 Chicago World's Fair" at http://www.homepages.indiana.edu/020102/text/history1.html

p. 61, "good many of our": Weinstein and Gatell, *The Segregation Era,* p. 97.

p. 61, "Things came to such": Rubel, *The Coming Free,* p. 22.

p. 61, "adjustment and submission" and "the alleged inferiority": Du Bois, *Writings,* p. 398.

p. 62, "So far as Mr. Washington": ibid, p. 404.

p. 62, "complain, and to complain": "The Niagara Movement's Declaration of Principles, 1905," at http://www.math.buffalo.edu/~sww/0history/hwny-niagara-movement.html

p. 63, "To treat evil": Lewis, *W. E. B. Du Bois,* p. 371.

Chapter 6: The Far Horizon

p. 66, "means that he": Booker T. Washington, "My View of Segregation Laws," *The New Republic*, December 4, 1915, at
http://teachingamericanhistory.org/library/index.asp?document=1152

p. 67, "justice done": Franklin and Moss, *From Slavery to Freedom*, p. 358.

p. 70, "to have a good": Litwack, *Trouble in Mind*, p. 56.

p. 71, "How shall we protect": ibid., pp. 318-319.

p. 71, "Courage! Look out": James Weldon Johnson, *Fifty Years and Other Poems*, at http://www.gutenberg.org/etext/17884

Index

Page numbers for illustrations are in boldface

accommodationism, 58, 61, 63, 66

Adams, Henry, 17

anti-lynching campaign, 48-50, **49**

Atlanta Compromise speech, 57-58, 60, 62

Black Codes, 25

black community
    black buisness owners, 65, **65**, 70, **70**
    black middle class, 70-71, **71**
    black newspapers, 70
    churches in, 69
    organizations for men and women, 67-68, 69
    schools in, 70
    writers and editors, 70

boycotts, 68

Brown, Ed, 40

children, black
    black schools, 36-39, **37**, **38**, 56, **57**, 58, 59, 70
    first encounters with Jim Crow, 33-34, 39-40

Church, Robert and Mary, 33-34

civil rights of African Americans, protecting, 26, **42**, 43, 67-68

Cobb, Ned, 41, 42

Constitution, U.S.

Fourteenth Amendment, 29, 30

Fifteenth Amendment, 26

convict leasing, 51-52

Declaration of Principles, 62

disenfranchising blacks, 26-28

Douglass, Frederick, 60, **60**

DuBois, W. E. B., 9, 35-36, 59, **59**, 61-62

education
    black educators, **54**, 55-59, **59**, 61-62
    black schools, 36-39, **37**, **38**, 56, **57**, 58, 59, 70
    illiteracy, 65
    industrial education, 56, 58, 61

Emancipation Proclamation, fiftieth anniversary (Jubilee) of, 65, 72

Exodus of 1879, 16, 20

Exodusters, 16-20, **19**

"Fifty Years" (Johnson), 71-72

Fisk University, 59

Free Speech, 48

gerrymandering, 27

Green, Ely, 39

Hampton Institute, 56

Harlan, John Marshall, 31, **31**

Harvard University, 59
Hayes, Rutherford B., 9, 12
Holsey, Albon, 40
Homestead Act of 1862, 16

Jim Crow system, **22**, 23, 25
    assault on voting rights, 26-28, **27**
    black schools and, 36-39, **37**, **38**
    churches in the Jim Crow era, 69
    in court, 50-52, **50**, **51**
    first encounters with, 39-40
    Jim Crow song, 24, **24**
    legal restrictions of, **32**, 34-36, **35**, 40
    lynchings, **44**, 45-50, **46**, **47**, **48**
    Plessy v. *Ferguson*, 28-31, **31**
    roots of segregation, 25-26, **25**
    struggles against, 67-68, 72
    surviving, 41-43, **41**
    unwritten laws of behavior, 40
Johnson, James Weldon, 71-72

Kansas, black migration to, 15-20, **16**, **17**
Ku Klux Klan (KKK), 8

Lewis, John Solomon, 11, 13, 14-15, 18
literacy tests, 27, **27**
lynchings, **44**, 45-50, **46**, **47**, **48**, 67,
    68, **68**

McCabe, Edwin, 17
Mays, Benjamin Elijah, 39-40, 41, 50
migrants, Southern black, **8**, 13-21, **14**,
    17, **19**, **21**
Moss, Thomas, 47-48, 49
Moton, Robert Russa, 39

National Association for the Advance-
    ment of Colored People (NAACP),
    62-63, **63**, 67
National Association of Colored Women
    (NACW), 67-68
Native Americans, 16
"New Negroes," 41-42, 46

New York Times, 72
newspapers, black, 70
Niagara Movement, 62-63

Ovington, Mary White, 63

Penn, W. F., 71
Plessy, Homer, 29
Plessy v. *Ferguson*, 28-31, **31**
poll tax, 27
public transportation laws, 28-31, **31**,
    35-36, 48

race riots, 52-53, **53**, 63
racism, 65, 67, 72
Reconstruction, 7-9, **8**
    black migration following end of,
        13-14, **14**
    dismantling achievements of, 23
    and repeal of Black Codes, 25
    and restoration of old slave system,
        12
    school segregation at end of, 36
    and voting rights, 27
Rice, Thomas Dartmouth, 24, **24**
Robinson, James, 39
Roosevelt, Theodore, 58-59, **59**
Ruffin, Josephine, 68

segregation
    American government and racist
        policies, 67
    Booker T. Washington on, 66
    boycotts against, 68
    introducing, **32**, 34-36, **35**
    Plessy v. *Ferguson*, 28-31, **31**
    roots of, **6**, 25-26, **25**
    school, 36-39, **37**, **38**
separate but equal doctrine, 30
Separate Car Acts, 29-30, 48
separate facilities, for blacks and whites,
    22, **32**, 34-36, **35**, 67
sharecroppers, **10**, 11

sharecropping system, 12-15, **12**
Singleton, Benjamin, 17
Souls of Black Folk, The (DuBois), 61
Supreme Court, U.S., 30, 31

temperance movement, 69
Terrell, Mary Church, **42**, 43, 68
Terrell, Robert, 43
Tourgée, Albion, 29-30
Tubman, Harriet, **67**, 68
Tuskegee Institute, **38**, 56, **57**, 58, 61

unions, black, 68
urban race wars, 52-53, **53**

Vardaman, James K., 38
voting rights, 26-28, **27**, 61
    women's suffrage, 68, 69

Walling, William English, 53
Washington, Booker T., **54**, 55-59, **59**, 60,
    61-62, **66**
    accommodationist policies, 58, 61,
        63, 66
    Atlanta Compromise speech, 57-
        58, 60, 62
    on segregation, 66
Wells, Ida B., 48-49, **49**, 68
White, George H., 28, **28**
white supremacy, 23, 26, 47, 48, 68
Wilson, Woodrow, 67
women, black
    civil rights advocate, **42**, 43, 68
    nursemaid, **13**
    organizations for, 67-68, 69
    pioneer family, **21**
    women's suffrage, 68, 69

About the Authors

JAMES HASKINS was professor of English at the University of Florida and lived in Gainesville, Florida, and New York City. Author of more than one hundred books for adults, young adults, and children, he received awards for his work in all three areas, including the John and Patricia Beatty Award of the California Library Association (2004), the *Washington Post* Children's Book Guild Award for his body of work in nonfiction for young people (1994), the Alabama Library Association Award for best work for children (1988), the ASCAP Deems Taylor Award for excellence in writing in the field of music (1979), and numerous Coretta Scott King and Carter G. Woodson awards.

KATHLEEN BENSON is curator of Community Projects at the Museum of the City of New York. She coedited the volume of essays *A Community of Many Worlds: Arab Americans in New York City* (2002) in connection with an exhibition of the same title, and coauthored several books with James Haskins, with whom she shared the ASCAP Deems Taylor Award (1979) for excellence in writing in the field of music.

VIRGINIA SCHOMP has written more than sixty titles for young readers on topics including dolphins, dinosaurs, occupations, American history, and world history, for which she has garnered much critical acclaim. She lives in the Catskill Mountain region of New York with her husband, Richard, and their son, Chip.